Benjamin Jowett

Socrates

The Apology and Crito of Plato

Benjamin Jowett

Socrates
The Apology and Crito of Plato

ISBN/EAN: 9783337102029

Printed in Europe, USA, Canada, Australia, Japan

Cover: Foto ©Thomas Meinert / pixelio.de

More available books at **www.hansebooks.com**

The Apology and Crito of Plato.

BOSTON:
Roberts Brothers.
1882.

Copyright, 1882,
BY ROBERTS BROTHERS.

UNIVERSITY PRESS:
JOHN WILSON AND SON, CAMBRIDGE.

CONTENTS.

	PAGE
INTRODUCTION	1
APOLOGY	21
CRITO	73

Introduction.

THE famous APOLOGY OF SOCRATES is here given, together with CRITO, in Professor Jowett's translation of Plato (the revised edition). The PHÆDO will soon follow in a companion volume. They are unabridged, and give the story of his trial, imprisonment, and death. In the following account of the life of Socrates I am largely indebted to an Introductory Essay to a translation of these Dialogues by Dean Church.

Socrates was born at Athens about the year 469 B.C. His father, Sophroniscus, was a sculptor, and Socrates himself practised the same art during his youth and early middle life. His mother, Phænarete, was a midwife. His parents, although poor, managed to give him the usual education. We know nothing definitely concerning him before the year 432 B.C., when he served as a hoplite, or heavy-armed foot-soldier, at the siege of Potidæa. He distinguished himself for bravery and endurance at this time, and also at the battle of Delium, 424 B. C., and at the battle of Amphipolis, 422 B. C.

Alcibiades describes his behavior when he was with him during the expedition to Potidæa. He says : [1] —

"There we messed together, and I had the opportunity of observing his extraordinary power of sustaining fatigue, and going without food when our supplies were intercepted at any place, as will happen with an army. In the faculty of endurance he was superior not only to me, but to everybody; there was no one to be compared to him. Yet at a festival he was the only person who had any real powers of enjoyment, and though not willing to drink, he could, if compelled, beat us all at that; and the most wonderful thing of all was that no human being had ever seen Socrates drunk. His endurance of cold was also surprising. There was a severe frost, for the winter in that region was really tremendous, and everybody else either remained indoors, or, if they went out, had on no end

[1] In the Symposium ; Jowett's translation.

Introduction. 3

of clothing, and were well shod, and had their feet swathed in felts and fleeces. In the midst of this Socrates, with his bare feet on the ice, and in his ordinary dress, marched better than any of the other soldiers who had their shoes on, and they looked daggers at him because he seemed to despise them.

"One morning he was thinking about something which he could not resolve; and he would not give up, but continued thinking from early dawn until noon. There he stood fixed in thought; and at noon attention was drawn to him, and the rumor ran through the wondering crowd that Socrates had been standing and thinking about something ever since the break of day. At last, in the evening after supper, some Ionians out of curiosity (I should explain that this was not in winter but in summer) brought out their mats and slept in the open air, that they might watch him, and see whether he would stand all night. There he stood all night as well as all day, and the following morning; and with the return of light he offered up a prayer to the sun, and went his way.

"I will also tell you, if you please, — and indeed I am bound to tell, — of his courage in battle; for who but he saved my life? Now this was the engagement in which I received the prize of valor; for I was wounded, and he would not leave me, but he rescued me and my arms; and he ought to have received the prize of valor, which the generals wanted to confer on me partly on account of my rank, and I told them so (this Socrates will not impeach or deny); but he was more eager than the generals that I, and not he, should have the prize.

"There was another occasion on which he was very noticeable: this was in the flight of the army after the battle of Delium; and I had a better opportunity of seeing him than at Potidæa, as I was myself on horseback, and therefore comparatively out of danger. He and Laches were retreating, as the troops were in flight, and I met them and told them not to be discouraged, and promised to remain with them. And there you might see him, Aristophanes, as you describe, just as he is in the streets of Athens, stalking like a pelican, and rolling his eyes, calmly contemplating enemies as well as friends, and making very intelligible to anybody, even from a distance, that whoever attacks him will be likely to meet with a stout resistance. And in this way he and his companion escaped,—for these are the sort of persons who are never touched in war; they only pursue those who are running away headlong. I particularly observed how superior he was to Laches in presence of mind.

"Many are the wonders of Socrates which I might narrate in his praise. Most of his ways might perhaps be paralleled in others, but the most astonishing thing of all is his absolute unlikeness to any human being that is or ever has been. You may imagine Brasidas and others to have been like Achilles; or you may imagine Nestor and Antenor to have been like Pericles; and the same may be said of other famous men: but of this strange being you will never be able to find any likeness, however remote, either among men who now are or who ever have been, except that which I have already suggested of Silenus and the satyrs;[1] and this is an allegory not only of himself, but also of his words. For, although I forgot to mention this before, his words are ridiculous when you first hear them; he clothes himself in language that is

[1] See p. 12.

as the skin of the wanton satyr : for his talk is of pack-asses and smiths and cobblers and curriers ; and he is always repeating the same things in the same words, so that an ignorant man who did not know him might feel disposed to laugh at him. But he who pierces the mask and sees what is within will find that they are the only words which have a meaning in them, and also the most divine, abounding in fair examples of virtue, and of the largest discourse, or rather extending to the whole duty of a good and honorable man."

His courage as a senator was even more remarkable than his courage as a soldier.

"In the year 406 B. C., the Athenian fleet defeated the Lacedæmonians at the battle of Arginusæ. After the battle the Athenian commanders neglected to recover the bodies of the dead and to save the living from their own disabled triremes. They said that they had ordered certain inferior officers to perform the duty, and that a storm had come on which had rendered the performance impossible. So the living were left to perish, and the bodies of the dead were never recovered. The Athenians, on receiving this news, were excessively angered. The due performance of funeral rites was a sacred duty with the Greeks, and many were indignant that their friends and relatives had been left to drown. There was a debate in the Assembly on the whole question, in which the commanders spoke, and it was resolved that the Senate should decide in what mode they should be tried. The Senate resolved by a majority that the Athenian people, having heard the accusation and the defence, should proceed to vote for the condemnation or acquittal of the eight commanders collectively, — an illegal proposal, because there was a law at Athens that on all trials a separate verdict should be found for each party accused.

"Socrates at that time was a member of the Senate, the only public office that he ever held. The Senate consisted of fifty men elected by lot from each of the ten tribes. Each tribe held the Prytany, or presidency, for thirty-five days at a time, and ten out of the fifty were presidents every seven days in succession. One of the ten held the supreme post each day, and for one day only. He was called Epistates; he laid all business before the Assembly; in short, he presided.

"On the day when it was proposed to take

a collective verdict on the eight commanders, Socrates happened to be Epistates. The proposal was illegal, though the fury of the people made it a very popular one. Some of the presidents refused to put such a question to the Assembly; but they were silenced by threats, and subsided. Socrates alone refused to submit or to put a question which he knew to be illegal. Threats of suspension and arrest, the clamor of a furious populace, the fear of death or imprisonment could not move him. 'I thought it my duty to face the danger out in the cause of law and justice, and not to be an accomplice in your unjust proposals.' But his authority lasted only for a day: a more pliant Epistates succeeded, and the commanders were condemned and executed.

"Two years later Socrates again showed by his conduct that he was ready to endure anything rather than do wrong. In 404 B.C. Athens was captured by the Lacedæmonians, and the long walls were thrown down. The great Athenian democracy was destroyed, and an oligarchy of Thirty set up in its place by Critias and others, with the help of the Spartan general, Lysander. The rule of the Thirty lasted for about a year (till the spring of 403

B. C.), and then the democracy was restored. The reign of Critias and his friends was a kind of reign of terror. Political opponents were murdered of course. So were respectable men, and wealthy men whose riches were desirable. All kinds of men were used as assassins, for the tyrants wished to implicate as many persons as possible in their crimes. With that design they sent for Socrates and four others to the Rotunda, — a building where the Prytanes took their meals, — and ordered them to bring over Leon, a native of Salamis, from that island to Athens, that they might kill him. To disobey the order probably meant death; and so reasoned the other four, who went over to Salamis and brought Leon across. Socrates disregarded the danger, and went quietly home. 'I showed not by words, but by actions that I did not care a straw about death; but that I did care very much about doing nothing wrong or wicked.' Fortunately he was saved by the destruction of the oligarchy." [1]

The date of his marriage to Xanthippe, whose violent temper has made her name a synonym for shrew, is unknown. She bore him three sons, named Lamprocles, Sophroniscus, and

[1] F. J. Church.

Menexenus. He gave a playful explanation of his choice, by remarking that "Those who wish to become skilled in horsemanship select the most spirited horses; after being able to bridle those, they believe they can bridle all others. Now as it is my wish to live and converse with men, I married this woman, being firmly convinced that in case I should be able to endure her, I should be able to endure all others."

"At what time Socrates relinquished his profession as a statuary we do not know," says Mr. Grote; "but it is certain that all the middle and later part of his life, at least, was devoted exclusively to the self-imposed task of teaching, excluding all other business, public or private, and to the neglect of all means of fortune. Early in the morning he frequented the public walks, the gymnasia for bodily training, and the schools where youths were receiving instruction. He was to be seen in the marketplace at the hour when it was most crowded, among the booths and tables where goods were exposed for sale. His whole day was usually spent in this manner. He talked with any one, young or old, rich or poor, who sought to address him, and in the hearing of all who chose to stand by; not only he never either asked or received any reward, but he made no distinction of persons, never withheld his conversation from any one, and talked upon the same general topics to all. He conversed with politicians, sophists, military men, artisans, ambitious or studious youths, etc. Nothing could be more public, perpetual, and indiscriminate as to persons than his conversation. But as it was engaging, curious, and instructive to hear, certain persons made it their habit to attend him in public as companions and listeners. These men, a fluctuating body, were commonly known as his disciples or scholars; though neither he nor his personal friends ever employed the terms *teacher* and *disciple* to describe the relation between them. Many of them came, attracted by his reputation, during the later years of his life, from other Grecian cities, Megara, Thebes, Elis, Cyrene, etc."

Alcibiades thus describes his eloquence: [1] " I shall praise Socrates in a figure which will appear to him to be a caricature, and yet I do not mean to laugh at him, but only to speak the truth. I say, then, that he is exactly like

[1] In the Symposium.

the masks of Silenus which may be seen sitting in the statuaries' shops, having pipes and flutes in their mouths; and they are made to open in the middle, and there are images of gods inside them. I say also that he is like Marsyas the satyr. You will not deny, Socrates, that your face is like that of a satyr. Aye, and there is a resemblance in other points too. For example, you are a bully: that I am in a position to prove by the evidence of witnesses, if you will not confess. And are you not a flute-player? That you are, and a far more wonderful performer than Marsyas. For he, indeed, with instruments charmed the souls of men by the power of his breath, as the performers of his music do still; for the melodies of Olympus are derived from the teaching of Marsyas, and these, whether they are played by a great master or by a miserable flute-girl, have a power which no others have: they alone possess the soul, and reveal the wants of those who have need of gods and mysteries, because they are inspired. But you produce the same effect with the voice only, and do not require the flute: that is the difference between you and him. When we hear any other speaker, even a very good one,

Introduction.

his words produce absolutely no effect upon us in comparison, whereas the very fragments of you and your words, even at second-hand, and however imperfectly repeated, amaze and possess the souls of every man, woman, and child who comes within hearing of them; and if I were not afraid that you would think me drunk, I would have sworn as well as spoken to the influence which they have always had and still have over me. For my heart leaps within me more than that of any Corybantian reveller, and my eyes rain tears when I hear them. And I observe that many others are affected in the same way. I have heard Pericles and other great orators, but though I thought that they spoke well, I never had any similar feeling; my soul was not stirred by them, nor was I angry at the thought of my own slavish state. But this Marsyas has often brought me to such a pass that I have felt as if I could hardly endure the life which I am leading (this, Socrates, you admit); and I am conscious that if I did not shut my ears against him, and fly from the voice of the siren, he would detain me until I grew old sitting at his feet. For he makes me confess that I ought not to live as I do, neglecting the wants of my own soul, and busying myself with the concerns of the Athenians, therefore I hold my ears and tear myself away from him. And he is the only person who ever made me ashamed,—which you might think not to be in my nature,—and there is no one else who does the same. For I know that I cannot answer him, or say that I ought not to do as he bids; but when I leave his presence the love of popularity gets the better of me. And therefore I run away and fly from him, and when I see him I am ashamed of what I have confessed to him. And many a time I wish that he were dead, and yet I know that I should be much more sorry than glad, if he were to die: so that I am at my wits' end."

Dean Church says:—"We now come to the trial and the defence of Socrates. He was indicted for impiety, and for corrupting young men, before a court of probably five hundred and one dicasts or judges. Multiply an English jury by about forty and take away the presiding judge, and we have such a court as that which tried Socrates: only we must add that the Athenian dicasts were a very animated audience, and were wont to express openly their pleasure or displeasure with what

Introduction. 15

was said. Socrates is often obliged to request them not to interrupt him; for the request is addressed to them, not to the general audience. The indictment was preferred by a young poet named Meletus, backed up by Lycon, a rhetorician of whom nothing more is known, and the real mover in the matter, Anytus. He was a leather-seller by trade, and he had acquired great influence and reputation with the people by his zeal and sufferings in the cause of democracy at the time of the oligarchy of the Thirty."

Grote says that Socrates, observing considerable intellectual promise in the son of Anytus, endeavored to dissuade the father from bringing him up to his own trade. As he had just sustained great loss of property, he was the more anxious that his son should labor to restore the family fortunes, and he naturally disliked interference with his plans. He also seems to have been an enemy of all teaching which went beyond the narrowest practicality. All three accusers belonged to classes which Socrates had irritated and offended.

"Some few words are necessary to explain the procedure at the trial. The time assigned to it was divided into three equal lengths. In the first the accusers—in the present instance all three of them—made their speeches; but with this we are not concerned. The second was occupied by the speech in defence. After that, the judges voted, and found the accused guilty or not guilty. The third length opened with the speech of the prosecutor advocating the penalty which he proposed,—in this instance death. The accused was at liberty to propose a lighter penalty, and he would then make a second speech in support of his proposal; he might at the same time appeal to the feelings of the court by bringing forward his wife and children. Then the judges would have to decide between the two penalties proposed to them, of which they had to select one. If they voted for death, the condemned man was led away to prison by the officers of the Eleven. The end of the Apology is not part of the trial, and we cannot be certain that Socrates was actually allowed to make such a farewell address. It must be at least doubtful whether those who had just condemned a man to death that they might be no longer made to give an account of their lives, would endure to hear him denouncing judgment against them for their sin, and prophesying the punishment which awaited them. Finally, we must remember that at certain points of his defence, properly so called, Socrates must be supposed to call witnesses to prove his statements."[1]

Professor Jowett says:—

"In what relation the Apology of Plato stands to the real defence of Socrates there are no means of determining. . . . But in the main it must be regarded as the ideal of Socrates, according to Plato's conception of him, appearing in the greatest and most public scene of his life, and in the height of his triumph, when he is weakest, and yet his mastery over mankind is greatest, and his habitual irony acquires a new meaning and a sort of tragic pathos in the face of death. The facts of his life are summed up, and the features of his character are brought out as if by accident in the course of the defence. The conversational manner, the seeming want of arrangement, the ironical simplicity, are found to result in a perfect work of art, which is the portrait of Socrates.

"Yet some of the topics may have been actually used by Socrates; and the recollection

[1] F. J. Church.

of his very words may have rung in the ears of his disciple."

Socrates was not put to death immediately, but remained in prison in chains about thirty days. One of his friends, Crito, comes to him the eve of the day when he is to die, to propose escape. It can be easily arranged, and he can be carried away in safety to another land, to end his days in peace. Socrates refuses to consent to such a plan, and the Dialogue of Crito contains his arguments against his friend.

In the Phædo the story of Socrates' death is told to Echecrates of Phlius, by Phædo, a favorite disciple, who had continued with his master to the end. He relates the long conversation of Socrates with his friends on the subject of immortality, and gives an account of his last hours, his calmness, his playfulness, and his quiet acceptance of the poison.

Xenophon says:[1] " Of those who knew what sort of man Socrates was, such as were lovers of virtue continue to regret him above all other men, even to the present day, as having contributed in the highest degree to their advancement in goodness. To me,

[1] Memorabilia.

being such as I have described him, — so pious that he did nothing without the sanction of the gods; so just that he wronged no man even in the most trifling affair, but was of service, in the most important matters, to those who enjoyed his society; so temperate that he never preferred pleasure to virtue; so wise that he never erred in distinguishing better from worse, needing no counsel from others, but being sufficient in himself to discriminate between them; so able to explain and settle such questions by argument; and so capable of discerning the character of others, of confuting those who were in error, and of exhorting them to virtue and honor, — he seemed to be such as the best and happiest of men would be. But if any one disapproves of my opinion, let him compare the conduct of others with that of Socrates, and determine accordingly."

M. W. T.

Apology.

HOW you, O Athenians, have been affected by my accusers, I cannot tell; but I know that they almost made me forget myself, so persuasively did they speak. And yet they have hardly uttered a word of truth. But many as their falsehoods were, there was one of them which quite amazed me; I mean when they told you that you should be upon your guard, and not allow yourselves to be deceived by my eloquence. To use such language, when they were sure to be detected as soon as I opened my lips and displayed my deficiency, did certainly appear most shameless, — unless by the force of eloquence they mean the force of truth; for if this is their meaning, I admit that I am eloquent. But in how different a way from theirs! Well, as I was saying, they have hardly uttered a word, or not more than a word, of truth;

but you shall hear from me the whole truth; not, however, delivered after their manner in a set oration duly ornamented with words and phrases. No, by heaven! but I shall use the words and arguments which occur to me at the moment; for I am certain that I am right in this, and that at my time of life I ought not to be appearing before you, O men of Athens, in the character of a juvenile orator, — let no one expect it of me. And I must beg of you to grant me a favor. If you hear me using the same words in my defence which I have been in the habit of using, and which most of you may have heard in the Agora, and at the tables of the money-changers, or anywhere else, I would ask you not to be surprised, and not to interrupt me on this account. For I am more than seventy years of age, and appearing now for the first time in a court of law, I am quite a stranger to the language which is used here; and therefore I would have you regard me as if I were really a stranger, whom you would excuse if he spoke in his native tongue, and after the fashion of his country. Am I making an unfair request of you? Never mind the manner, which may or may not be good; but think only of the justice of my cause, and give heed to that: let the judge decide justly and the speaker speak truly.

And first, I have to reply to the older charges and to my first accusers, and then I will go on to the later ones. For of old I have had many accusers, who have accused me falsely to you during many years; and I am more afraid of them than of Anytus and his associates, who are dangerous too, in their own way. But far more dangerous are the others, who began when you were children, and took possession of your minds with their falsehoods, telling of one Socrates, a wise man, who speculated about the heaven above, and searched into the earth beneath, and made the worse appear the better cause. The disseminators of this tale are the accusers whom I dread; for their hearers are apt to fancy that such inquirers do not believe in the existence of the gods. And they are many, and their charges against me are of ancient date, and they made them in days when you were impressible, — in childhood, or perhaps in youth, — and the cause when heard went by default, for there was none to answer. And, hardest of all, their names I do not know and cannot tell, unless in the chance case of a comic poet. But the main body of these slanderers, who from envy and malice have wrought upon you,— and there are some of them who are convinced themselves and impart their convictions to others, — all this class of men are most difficult to deal with ; for I cannot have them up here and examine them, and therefore I must simply fight with shadows in my own defence, and examine when there is no one who answers. I will ask you, then, to assume with me, as I was saying, that my opponents are of two kinds, — one recent, the other ancient, — and I hope that you will see the propriety of my answering the latter first, for these accusations you heard long before the others, and much oftener.

Well, then, I must make my defence, and endeavor to clear away in a short time a slander which has lasted a long time ; and I hope that I may succeed, and that my words may find favor with you, if this be well for you and me. But I know that to accomplish this is not easy. I quite see the nature of the task. Let the event be as God wills ; in obedience to the law I make my defence.

I will begin at the beginning, and ask what

the accusation is which has given rise to this slander of me, and which encouraged Meletus to proceed against me. Well, what do the slanderers say? They shall be my prosecutors, and I will sum up their words in an affidavit: "Socrates is an evil-doer and a curious person, who searches into things under the earth and in heaven, and he makes the worse appear the better cause; and he teaches the aforesaid doctrines to others." Such is the accusation, and is just what you have yourselves seen in the comedy of Aristophanes, who has introduced a man, whom he calls Socrates, going about and saying that he can walk in the air, and talking a deal of nonsense concerning matters of which I do not pretend to know either much or little, — not that I mean to speak disparagingly of any one who is a student of natural philosophy. I should be very sorry if Meletus could lay that to my charge. But the simple truth is, O Athenians, that I have nothing to do with physical speculations. Very many of those here present are witnesses to the truth of this, and to them I appeal. Speak, then, you who have heard me, and tell your neighbors whether any of you have ever known me hold forth, in few words or in many, upon such matters. . . . You hear their answer; and from what they say of this part of the charge you will be able to judge of the truth of the rest.

As little foundation is there for the report that I am a teacher, and take money: that is no more true than the other. Although, if a man were really able to instruct mankind, to take money for giving instruction would, in my opinion, be honorable. There is Gorgias of Leontium, and Prodicus of Ceos, and Hippias of Elis, who go the round of the cities, and are able to persuade the young men to leave their own citizens, by whom they might be taught for nothing, and come to them, whom they not only pay, but are thankful if they may be allowed to pay them.

There is at this time a Parian philosopher residing in Athens, of whom I have heard; and I came to hear of him in this way: I met a man who has spent a world of money on the Sophists, Callias, the son of Hipponicus, and knowing that he had sons, I asked him: Callias, I said, if your two sons were foals or calves, there would be no difficulty in finding some one to put over them; we should hire a trainer of horses, or a farmer, probably, who would improve and perfect them in their own proper virtue and excellence; but as they are human beings, whom are you thinking of placing over them? Is there any one who understands human and political virtue? You must have thought about the matter, for you have sons; is there any one? "There is," he said. Who is he? said I; and of what country? and what does he charge? "Evenus the Parian," he replied; "he is the man, and his charge is five minæ!" Happy is Evenus, I said to myself, if he really has this wisdom and teaches at such a modest charge. Had I the same, I should have been very proud and satisfied; but the truth is that I have no knowledge of the kind.

I dare say, Athenians, that some one among you will reply, "Yes, Socrates, but what is the origin of these accusations which are brought against you? — there must have been something strange which you have been doing. All this rumor and talk about you would never have arisen if you had been like other men. Tell us, then, what is the cause of them, for we should be sorry to judge hastily of you." Now I regard this as a fair challenge, and I will endeavor to explain to you the origin of this name of "wise," and of my evil fame. Please to attend, then. And although some of you may think that I am joking, I declare that I will tell you the entire truth. Men of Athens, this reputation of mine has come of a certain sort of wisdom which I possess. If you ask me what kind of wisdom, I reply, such wisdom as is attainable by man, for to that extent I am inclined to believe that I am wise; whereas the persons of whom I was speaking have a superhuman wisdom, which I may fail to describe, because I have it not myself; and he who says that I have, speaks falsely, and is taking away my character. And here, O men of Athens, I must beg you not to interrupt me, even if I seem to say something extravagant. For the word which I will speak is not mine. I will refer you to a witness who is worthy of credit, and will tell you about my wisdom, — whether I have any, and of what sort, — and that witness shall be the God of Delphi. You must have known Chærephon; he was early a friend of mine, and also a friend of yours, for he shared in the exile of the people, and returned with you. Well, Chærephon, as you know, was very impetuous in all his doings, and he went to Delphi and boldly asked the oracle to tell him whether, — as I was saying, I must beg you not to interrupt, — he asked the oracle to tell him whether there was any one wiser than I was, and the Pythian prophetess answered that there was no man wiser. Chærephon is dead himself, but his brother, who is in court, will confirm the truth of what I am saying.

Why do I mention this? Because I am going to explain to you why I have such an evil name. When I heard the answer, I said to myself, "What can the God mean? and what is the interpretation of his riddle? for I know that I have no wisdom, small or great. What, then, can he mean when he says that I am the wisest of men? And yet he is a god, and cannot lie; that would be against his nature."

After long consideration, I at last thought of a method of trying the question. I reflected that if I could only find a man wiser than myself, then I might go to the God with a refutation in my hand. I should say to him, "Here is a man who is wiser than I am; but you said that I was the wisest!" Accordingly I went to one who had the reputation of wisdom, and observed him, — his name I need not mention; he was a politician whom I selected for examination, and the result was as follows: —

When I began to talk with him, I could not help thinking that he was not really wise, although he was thought wise by many, and wiser still by himself; and thereupon I tried to explain to him that he thought himself wise, but was not really wise; and the consequence was that he hated me, and his enmity was shared by several who were present and heard me. So I left him, saying to myself as I went away: Well, although I do not suppose that either of us knows anything really beautiful and good, I am better off than he is, — for he knows nothing and thinks that he knows; I neither know nor think that I know. In this latter particular, then, I seem to have slightly the advantage of him. Then I went to another, who had still higher philosophical pretensions, and my conclusion was exactly the same. I made another enemy of him, and of many others besides him.

Then I went to one man after another, being not unconscious of the enmity which I provoked, and I lamented and feared this. But necessity was laid upon me: the word of

God, I thought, ought to be considered first. And I said to myself: Go I must to all who appear to know, and find out the meaning of the oracle. And I swear to you, Athenians, by the dog I swear!—for I must tell you the truth—the result of my mission was just this: I found that the men most in repute were all but the most foolish; and that some inferior men were really wiser and better. I will tell you the tale of my wanderings and of the "Herculean" labors, as I may call them, which I endured, only to find at last the oracle irrefutable. When I left the politicians I went to the poets, — tragic, dithyrambic, and all sorts. And there, I said to myself, you will be instantly detected; now you will find out that you are more ignorant than they are. Accordingly, I took them some of the most elaborate passages in their own writings, and asked what was the meaning of them,—thinking that they would teach me something. Will you believe me? I am almost ashamed to confess the truth, but I must say that there is hardly a person present who would not have talked better about their poetry than they did themselves. Then I knew without going further that not by wisdom do poets write poetry, but by a sort of genius and inspiration; they are like diviners or soothsayers, who also say many fine things, but do not understand the meaning of them. And the poets appeared to me to be much in the same case; and I further observed that upon the strength of their poetry they believed themselves to be the wisest of men in other things in which they were not wise. So I departed, conceiving myself to be superior to them for the same reason that I was superior to the politicians.

At last I went to the artisans, for I was conscious that I knew nothing at all, as I may say, and I was sure that they knew many fine things; and here I was not mistaken, for they did know many things of which I was ignorant, and in this they were certainly wiser than I was. But I observed that even the good artisans fell into the same error as the poets: because they were good workmen they thought that they also knew all sorts of high matters, and this defect in them overshadowed their wisdom. Therefore I asked myself on behalf of the oracle whether I would like to be as I was, neither having their knowledge nor their ignorance, or like them in both;

and I made answer to myself and the oracle that I was better off as I was.

This investigation has led to my having many enemies of the worst and most dangerous kind, and has given occasion also to many calumnies. And I am called wise, for my hearers always imagine that I myself possess the wisdom which I find wanting in others. But the truth is, O men of Athens, that God only is wise; and in his answer he means to say that the wisdom of men is little or nothing. He is not speaking of Socrates, he is only using my name by way of illustration, as if he said, He, O men, is the wisest who, like Socrates, knows that his wisdom is in truth worth nothing. And so I go my way, obedient to the god, and make inquisition into the wisdom of any one, whether citizen or stranger, who appears to be wise; and if he is not wise, then, in vindication of the oracle, I show him that he is not wise. And my occupation quite absorbs me, and I have no time to give either to any public matter of interest or to any concern of my own, but I am in utter poverty by reason of my devotion to the god.

There is another thing: Young men of

the richer classes, who have not much to do, come about me of their own accord. They like to hear the pretenders examined, and they often imitate me and proceed to examine others. There are plenty of persons, as they soon enough discover, who think that they know something, but really know little or nothing; and then those who are examined by them, instead of being angry with themselves, are angry with me. This confounded Socrates, they say; this villanous misleader of youth! And then if somebody asks them, Why, what evil does he practise or teach? they do not know, and cannot tell. But in order that they may not appear to be at a loss, they repeat the ready-made charges which are used against all philosophers, about teaching things up in the clouds and under the earth, and having no gods, and making the worse appear the better cause; for they do not like to confess that their pretence of knowledge has been detected — which is the truth. And as they are numerous and ambitious and energetic, and are drawn up in battle array and have persuasive tongues, they have filled your ears with their loud and inveterate calumnies. And this is the reason why my three accusers, Meletus and Anytus and Lycon, have set upon me, — Meletus, who has a quarrel with me on behalf of the poets; Anytus, on behalf of the craftsmen; Lycon, on behalf of the rhetorician. And, as I said at the beginning, I cannot expect to get rid of such a mass of calumny all in a moment. And this, O men of Athens, is the truth and the whole truth: I have concealed nothing, I have dissembled nothing. And yet I know that my plainness of speech makes them hate me; and what is their hatred but a proof that I am speaking the truth? This is the occasion and reason of their slander of me, as you will find out either in this or in any future inquiry.

I have said enough in my defence against the first class of my accusers: I turn to the second class, who are headed by Meletus, that good and patriotic man, as he calls himself. And now I will try to defend myself against them: these new accusers must also have their affidavit read. What do they say? Something of this sort: That Socrates is a doer of evil, and a corruptor of the youth; he does not believe in the gods of the state, and has other new divinities of his own. That is the sort of charge; and now let us examine the particular counts. He says that I am a doer of evil, who corrupt the youth; but I say, O men of Athens, that Meletus is a doer of evil, and the evil is that he mixes up jest and earnest, and is too ready at bringing other men to trial from a pretended zeal and interest about matters in which he really never had the smallest interest. And the truth of this I will endeavor to prove.

Come hither, Meletus, and let me ask a question of you. You think a great deal about the improvement of youth?

Yes, I do.

Tell the judges, then, who is their improver; for you must know, as you have taken the pains to discover their corruptor, and are citing and accusing me before them. Speak, then, and tell the judges who their improver is. Observe, Meletus, that you are silent, and have nothing to say. But is not this rather disgraceful, and a very considerable proof of what I was saying, that you have no interest in the matter? Speak up, friend, and tell us who their improver is.

The laws.

But that, my good sir, is not my meaning.

I want to know who the person is who, in the first place, knows the laws.

The judges, Socrates, who are present in court.

What! do you mean to say, Meletus, that they are able to instruct and improve youth?

Certainly they are.

What! all of them, or some only, and not others?

All of them.

By the goddess Here, that is good news! There are plenty of improvers, then. And what do you say of the audience, — do they improve them?

Yes, they do.

And the senators?

Yes, the senators improve them.

But perhaps the members of the assembly corrupt them : or do they too improve them?

They improve them.

Then every Athenian improves and elevates them, all with the exception of myself; and I alone am their corruptor? Is that what you affirm?

That is what I stoutly affirm.

I am very unfortunate, if you are right. But suppose I ask you a question : Would you say that the same holds true in the case of horses? Does one man do them harm, and all the world good? Is not the exact opposite of this true? One man is able to do them good, or at least not many, — the trainer of horses, that is to say, does them good, and others who have to do with them rather injure them? Is not that true, Meletus, of horses, or any other animals? Yes, unmistakably; whether you and Anytus say yes or no. Happy indeed would be the condition of youth if they had one corruptor only, and all the rest of the world were their improvers. And you, Meletus, have sufficiently shown that you never had a thought about the young: your carelessness is seen in your not caring about the matters spoken of in your own indictment.

And now, Meletus, I must ask you another question: Which is better, to live among bad citizens or among good ones? Answer, friend, I say; for that is a question which may be easily answered. Do not the good do their neighbors good, and the bad do them evil?

Certainly.

And is there any one who would rather be injured than benefited by those who live with him? Answer, my good friend, the law requires you to answer. Does any one like to be injured?

Certainly not.

And when you accuse me of corrupting the youth, do you allege that I corrupt them intentionally, or unintentionally?

Intentionally, I say.

But you have just admitted that the good do their neighbors good, and the evil do them evil. Now is that a truth which your superior wisdom has recognized thus early in life, and am I at my age in such darkness and ignorance as not to know that if a man with whom I have to live is corrupted by me, I am very likely to be harmed by him; and yet I corrupt him, and intentionally too,—that is what you are saying, and of that you will never persuade me or any other human being. But either I do not corrupt them, or I corrupt them unintentionally; and so on either view of the case you lie. If my offence is unintentional, the law has no cognizance of unintentional offences; you ought to have taken me privately, and warned and admonished me; for if I had been better advised, I should have left off doing what I only did unintentionally, — no doubt I should, — whereas you hated to converse with me or teach me, but you indicted me in this court, which is a place not of instruction, but of punishment.

I have shown, Athenians, as I was saying, that Meletus has no care at all, great or small, about the matter. But still I should like to know, Meletus, in what I am affirmed to corrupt the young. I suppose you mean, as I infer from your indictment, that I teach them not to acknowledge the gods which the state acknowledges, but some other new divinities or spiritual agencies in their stead. These are the lessons which corrupt the youth, as you say.

Yes, that I say emphatically.

Then, by the gods, Meletus, of whom we are speaking, tell me and the court, in somewhat plainer terms, what you mean. For I do not as yet understand whether you affirm that I teach others to acknowledge some gods, and therefore do believe in gods, and am not an entire atheist, — this you do not lay to my charge, — but only that they are not the same gods which the city recognizes: the charge is that they are different gods. Or do you mean to say that I am an atheist simply, and a teacher of atheism?

Apology.   41

I mean the latter, that you are a complete atheist.

That is an extraordinary statement, Meletus. Why do you say that? Do you mean that I do not believe in the godhead of the sun or moon, which is the common creed of all men?

I assure you, judges, that he does not believe in them; for he says that the sun is stone, and the moon earth.

Friend Meletus, you think that you are accusing Anaxagoras; and you have but a bad opinion of the judges if you fancy them ignorant to such a degree as not to know that these doctrines are found in the books of Anaxagoras the Clazomenian, who is full of them. And these are the doctrines which the youth are said to learn of Socrates, when there are not unfrequently exhibitions of them at the theatre [1] (price of admission one drachma at the most); and they might cheaply purchase them, and laugh at Socrates if he pretends to father such remarkable views. And so, Meletus, you really think that I do not believe in any god?

[1] Probably in allusion to Aristophanes, who caricatured, and to Euripides who borrowed, the notions of Anaxagoras, as well as to other dramatic poets.

I swear by Zeus that you believe absolutely in none at all.

You are a liar, Meletus, not believed even by yourself. For I cannot help thinking, O men of Athens! that Meletus is reckless and impudent, and that he has written this indictment in a spirit of mere wantonness and youthful bravado. Has he not compounded a riddle, thinking to try me? He said to himself: I shall see whether the wise Socrates will discover my pleasant contradiction, or whether I shall be able to deceive him and the rest of them. For he certainly does appear to me to contradict himself in the indictment as much as if he said that Socrates is guilty of not believing in the gods, and yet of believing in them, — but this surely is a piece of fun.

I should like you, O men of Athens! to join me in examining what I conceive to be his inconsistency; and do you, Meletus, answer. And I must remind the audience that they are not to interrupt me if I speak in my accustomed manner.

Did ever man, Meletus, believe in the existence of human things, and not of human beings? — I wish, men of Athens, that he would answer, and not be always trying to get up an interruption.—Did ever any man believe in horsemanship, and not in horses? or in flute-playing, and not in flute-players? No, my friend; I will answer to you and to the court, as you refuse to answer for yourself. There is no man who ever did. But now please to answer the next question: Can a man believe in spiritual and divine agencies, and not in spirits or demigods?

He cannot.

I am glad that I have extracted that answer, by the assistance of the court; nevertheless you swear in the indictment that I teach and believe in divine or spiritual agencies (new or old, no matter for that); at any rate I believe in spiritual agencies, as you say and swear in the affidavit. But if I believe in divine beings, I must believe in spirits or demigods. Is not that true? Yes, that is true, for I may assume that your silence gives assent to that. Now what are spirits or demigods? Are they not either gods or the sons of gods? Is that true?

Yes, that is true.

But this is just the ingenious riddle of which I was speaking: the demigods or spirits are gods, and you say first that I do not believe in gods, and then again that I do believe in gods; that is, if I believe in demigods. For if the demigods are the illegitimate sons of gods, whether by the nymphs or by any other mothers, as is thought, that, as all men will allow, necessarily implies the existence of their parents. You might as well affirm the existence of mules, and deny that of horses and asses. Such nonsense, Meletus, could only have been intended by you as a trial of me. You have put this into the indictment because you had nothing real of which to accuse me. But no one who has a particle of understanding will ever be convinced by you that the same men can believe in divine and superhuman things, and yet not believe that there are gods and demigods and heroes.

I have said enough in answer to the charge of Meletus, — any elaborate defence is unnecessary. But, as I was saying before, I certainly have many enemies, and this is what will be my destruction if I am destroyed: of that I am certain: not Meletus, nor yet Anytus, but the envy and detraction of the world, which has been the death of many good men, and will probably be the death of many more: there is no danger of my being the last of them.

Some one will say: And are you not ashamed, Socrates, of a course of life which is likely to bring you to an untimely end? To him I may fairly answer: There you are mistaken: a man who is good for anything ought not to calculate the chance of living or dying; he ought only to consider whether, in doing anything, he is doing right or wrong, — acting the part of a good man or of a bad. Whereas, according to your view, the heroes who fell at Troy were not good for much, and the son of Thetis above all, who altogether despised danger in comparison with disgrace; and when his goddess mother said to him, in his eagerness to slay Hector, that if he avenged his companion Patroclus, and slew Hector, he would die himself. "Fate," as she said, "waits upon you next after Hector." He, hearing this, utterly despised danger and death, and instead of fearing them, feared rather to live in dishonor and not to avenge his friend. "Let me die next," he replies, "and be avenged of my enemy, rather than abide here by the beaked ships, a scorn and a burden of the earth." Had Achilles any thought of death and danger? For wherever a man's place is, whether the place which he has chosen or that in which he has been placed by a commander, there he ought to remain in the hour of danger; he should not think of death or of anything but of disgrace. And this, O men of Athens, is a true saying.

Strange indeed would be my conduct, O men of Athens, if I, who, when I was ordered by the generals whom you chose to command me at Potidæa and Amphipolis and Delium, remained where they placed me, like any other man, facing death, — if, I say, now, when, as I conceive and imagine, God orders me to fulfil the philosopher's mission of searching into myself and other men, I were to desert my post through fear of death or any other fear; that would indeed be strange, and I might justly be arraigned in court for denying the existence of the gods, if I disobeyed the oracle because I was afraid of death: then I should be fancying that I was wise when I was not wise. For the fear of death is indeed the pretence of wisdom, and not real wisdom, being a pretended knowledge of the unknown; and no one knows whether death, which men in their fear apprehend to be the greatest evil, may not be the greatest good. Is there not here conceit of knowledge, which is a disgraceful sort of ignorance? And this is the point in which, as I think, I differ from others, and in which I might perhaps fancy myself wiser than men in general, — that whereas I know but little of the world below, I do not suppose that I know; but I do know that injustice and disobedience to a better, whether God or man, is evil and dishonorable, and I will never fear or avoid a possible good rather than a certain evil. And therefore, if you let me go now, and reject the counsels of Anytus, who said that if I were not put to death I ought not to have been prosecuted, and that if I escape now your sons will all be utterly ruined by listening to my words, — if you say to me: Socrates, this time we will not mind Anytus, and will let you off; but upon one condition, that you are not to inquire and speculate in this way any more, and that if you are caught doing this again you shall die, — if this was the condition on which you let me go, I should reply :- Men of Athens, I honor and love you; but I shall obey God rather than you, and while I have life and strength I shall never cease from the practice and teaching of philosophy, exhorting any one whom I meet after my manner, and convincing him, saying: Oh, my friend, why do you, who are a citizen of the great and mighty and wise city of Athens, care so much about laying up the greatest amount of money and honor and reputation, and so little about wisdom and truth and the greatest improvement of the soul, which you never regard or heed at all? Are you not ashamed of this? And if the person with whom I am arguing says: Yes, but I do care, — I do not depart or let him go at once; I interrogate and examine and cross-examine him, and if I think that he has no virtue, but only says that he has, I reproach him with undervaluing the greater and overvaluing the less. And I say the same to every one whom I meet, young and old, citizen and alien, but especially to the citizens, inasmuch as they are my brethren. For know that this is the command of God, and I believe that to this day no greater good has ever happened in the state than my service to the God. For I do nothing but go about persuading you all, old and young alike, not to take thought for your persons or your properties, but first and chiefly to care about the greatest improvement of the soul. I tell you that virtue is not given by money, but that from virtue come money and every other good of man, public as well as private. This is my teaching, and if this is the doctrine which corrupts the youth, my influence is ruinous indeed. But if any one says that this is not my teaching, he is speaking an untruth. Wherefore, O men of Athens, I say to you, Do as Anytus bids, or not as Anytus bids, and either acquit me or not; but whatever you do, understand that I shall never alter my ways, not even if I have to die many times.

Men of Athens, do not interrupt, but hear me: there was an agreement between us that you should hear me out. And I think that what I am going to say will do you good; for I have something more to say, at which you may be inclined to cry out; but I beg that you will not. I would have you know that if you kill such an one as I am, you will injure yourselves more than you will injure me. Nothing will injure me, not Meletus, nor yet Anytus, — they cannot, for a bad man is not permitted to injure a better than himself. I do not deny that he may perhaps kill him, or drive him into exile, or deprive him of civil rights: and he may imagine, and others may imagine, that he is doing him a great injury: but in that I do not agree with him; for the evil of doing as Anytus is doing, — of unjustly taking away another man's life, — is greater far. And now, Athenians, I am not going to argue for my own sake, as you may think, but for yours, that you may not sin against the God, or lightly reject his boon by condemning me. For if you kill me you will not easily find another like me, who, if I may use such a ludicrous figure of speech, am a sort of gadfly given to the state by the God; and the state is like a great and noble steed who is tardy in his motions, owing to his very size, and requires to be stirred into life. I am that gadfly which God has given the state, and all day long and in all places am always fastening upon you, arousing and persuading and reproaching you. And as you will not easily find another like me, I would advise you to spare me. I dare say that you may feel irritated at being suddenly awakened when you are caught napping; and you may think that if you were to strike me dead as Anytus advises, which you easily might, then you would sleep on for the remainder of your lives, unless God in his care of you gave you another gadfly. And that I am given to you by God is proved by this: that if I had been like other men, I should not have neglected all my own concerns, or patiently seen the neglect of them during all these years, and have been doing yours, coming to you individually like a father or elder brother, exhorting you to regard virtue, — such conduct, I say, would be unlike human nature. And had I gained anything, or if my exhortations had been paid, there would have been some sense in that; but now, as you will perceive, not even the impudence of my accusers dares to say that I have ever exacted or sought pay of any one, — of that they have no witness. And I have a witness of the truth of what I say: my poverty is a sufficient witness.

Some one may wonder why I go about in private giving advice and busying myself with the concerns of others, but do not venture to come forward in public and advise the state. I will tell you why. You have often heard me speak in times past of an oracle or sign which comes to me, and is the divinity which Meletus ridicules in the indictment. This sign I have had ever since I was a child.

The sign is a voice which comes to me and always forbids me to do something which I am going to do, but never commands me to do anything, and this is what stands in the way of my being a politician. And rightly, as I think. For I am certain, O men of Athens, that if I had engaged in politics, I should have perished long ago, and done no good either to you or to myself. And do not be offended at my telling you the truth; for the truth is, that no man who goes to war with you or any other multitude, honestly struggling against the commission of unrighteousness and wrong in the state, will save his life: he who will really fight for the right, if he would live even for a little while, must have a private station, and not a public one.

I can give you as proofs of what I say, not words only, but deeds, which you value far more. Let me tell you a passage of my own life which will prove to you that I should never have yielded to injustice from any fear of death, and that when I refused to yield I must have died. I will tell you a tale of the courts, not very interesting perhaps, but nevertheless true. The only office of state which I ever held, O men of Athens, was that of senator. The tribe Antiochis, which is my tribe, had the presidency at the trial of the generals who had not taken up the bodies of the slain after the battle of Arginusæ, and you proposed to try them in a body, which was illegal, as you all thought afterwards. But at the time I was the only one of the Prytanes who was opposed to the illegality, and I gave my vote against you; and when the orators threatened to impeach and arrest me, and have me taken away, and you called and shouted, I made up my mind that I would run the risk, having law and justice with me, rather than take part in your injustice because I feared imprisonment and death. This happened in the days of the democracy. But when the oligarchy of the Thirty was in power, they sent for me and four others into the Rotunda, and bade us bring Leon the Salaminian from Salamis, as they wanted to execute him. That was a specimen of the sort of commands which they were always giving, with the view of implicating as many as possible in their crimes; and then I showed, not in word only, but in deed, that — if I may be allowed to use such an expression — I cared not a straw for death, and that my sole fear was the fear of doing an unrighteous or unholy thing. For the strong arm of that oppressive power did not frighten me into doing wrong. And when we came out of the Rotunda the other four went to Salamis and fetched Leon; but I went quietly home. For which I might have lost my life, had not the power of the Thirty shortly afterwards come to an end. And many will witness to my words.

Now do you really imagine that I could have survived all these years if I had led a public life, supposing that, like a good man, I had always supported the right and had made justice, as I ought, the first thing? No indeed, men of Athens, neither I nor any other. But I have been always the same in all my actions, public as well as private, and never have I yielded any base compliance to those who are slanderously termed my disciples, or to any other. For the truth is that I have no regular disciples; but if any one likes to come and hear me while I am pursuing my mission, whether he be young or old, he may freely come. Nor do I converse with those who pay only, and not with those who do not pay; but any one, whether he be rich or poor, may ask and answer me, and listen to my words;

and whether he turns out to be a bad man or a good one, that cannot be justly laid to my charge, as I never taught, or professed to teach him anything. And if any one says that he has ever learned or heard anything from me in private which all the world has not heard, I should like you to know that he is speaking an untruth.

But I shall be asked: Why do people delight in continually conversing with you? I have told you already, Athenians, the whole truth about this: they like to hear the cross-examination of the pretenders to wisdom; there is amusement in it. To converse with others is a duty which the God has imposed upon me, as I am assured by oracles, visions, and in every way in which the will of divine power was ever signified to any one. This is true, O Athenians, or if not true, would be soon refuted. For if I am really corrupting the youth, and have corrupted some of them already, those of them who have grown up and have become sensible that I gave them bad advice in the days of their youth should come forward as accusers and take their revenge. And if they do not like to come themselves, some of their relatives, fathers, brothers, or other kinsmen should say what evil their families suffered at my hands. Now is their time. Many of them I see in the court. There is Crito, who is of the same age and of the same deme with myself, and there is Critobulus, his son, whom I also see. Then again there is Lysanias of Sphettus, who is the father of Æschines, he is present; and also there is Antiphon of Cephisus, who is the father of Epigenes; and there are the brothers of several who have associated with me. There is Nicostratus, the son of Theosdotides and the brother of Theodotus (now Theodotus himself is dead, and therefore he, at any rate, will not seek to stop him); and there is Paralus, the son of Demodocus, who had a brother Theages; and Adeimantus, the son of Ariston, whose brother Plato is present; and Æantodorus, who is the brother of Apollodorus, whom I also see. I might mention a great many others, any of whom Meletus should have produced as witnesses in the course of his speech; and let him still produce them, if he has forgotten, — I will make way for him. And let him say if he has any testimony of the sort which he can produce. Nay, Athenians, the very opposite is the truth. For all these are ready to witness on behalf of the corruptor, of the destroyer of their kindred, as Meletus and Anytus call me; not the corrupted youth only, — there might have been a motive for that, — but their uncorrupted elder relatives. Why should they too support me with their testimony? Why, indeed, except for the sake of truth and justice, and because they know that I am speaking the truth, and that Meletus is lying?

Well, Athenians, this and the like of this is nearly all the defence which I have to offer. Yet a word more. Perhaps there may be some one who is offended at me when he calls to mind how he himself on a similar, or even a less serious occasion, had prayed and entreated the judges with many tears, and how he produced his children in court, which was a moving spectacle, together with a host of relations and friends: whereas I, who am probably in danger of my life, will do none of these things. The contrast may occur to his mind, and he may be set against me and vote in anger because he is displeased at me on this account. Now if there be such a person among you, — which I am far from affirming, — I may fairly reply to him: My friend, I am a man, and like other men, a creature of flesh and blood, and not "of wood or stone," as Homer says; and I have a family, yes, and sons, O Athenians, three in number, one of whom is growing up, and the two others are still young; and yet I will not bring any of them hither in order to petition you for an acquittal. And why not? Not from any self-will or disregard of you. Whether I am or am not afraid of death is another question, of which I will not now speak. But my reason simply is, that I feel such conduct to be discreditable to myself and to you and to the whole state. One who has reached my years and who has a name for wisdom, whether deserved or not, ought not to demean himself. At any rate the world has decided that Socrates is in some way superior to other men. And if those among you who are said to be superior in wisdom and courage, and any other virtue, demean themselves in this way, how shameful is their conduct! I have seen men of reputation, when they have been condemned, behaving in the strangest manner: they seemed to fancy that they were going to suffer something dreadful if they died, and that they could be immortal if you only allowed them to live; and I think that they were a dishonor to the state, and that any stranger coming in would have said of them that the most eminent men of Athens, to whom the Athenians themselves give honor and command, are no better than women. And I say that these things ought not to be done by those of us who are of reputation; and if they are done, you ought not to permit them; you ought rather to show that you are more inclined to condemn, not the man who is quiet, but the man who gets up a doleful scene, and makes the city ridiculous.

But, setting aside the question of dishonor, there seems to be something unjust in petitioning a judge, and thus procuring an acquittal instead of informing and convincing him. For his duty is, not to make a present of justice, but to give judgment; and he has sworn that he will judge according to the laws, and not according to his own good pleasure; and we ought not to encourage you, or you allow yourselves to be encouraged, in this habit of perjury — there can be no piety in that. Do not then require me to do what I consider dishonorable and impious and wrong, especially now, when I am being tried for impiety on the indictment of Meletus. For if, O men of Athens, by force of persuasion and entreaty I could overpower your oaths, then I should be teaching you to believe that there are no gods, and convict myself, in my own defence, of not believing in them. But that is not the case: for I do believe that there are gods, and in a far higher sense than that in which any of my accusers believe in them. And to you and to God I commit my cause, to be determined by you as is best for you and me.

[Socrates here concludes his defence, and, the votes being taken, he is declared guilty by a majority of voices. He thereupon resumes his address.]

There are many reasons why I am not grieved, O men of Athens, at the vote of condemnation. I expected it, and am only surprised that the votes are so nearly equal; for I had thought that the majority against me would have been far larger; but now, had three votes gone over to the other side, I should have been acquitted. And I may say, I think, that I have escaped Meletus. Nay, I may say more; for without the assistance of Anytus and Lycon, he would not have had a fifth part of the votes, as the law requires, in which case he would have incurred a fine of a thousand drachmæ, as is evident.

And so he proposes death as the penalty. And what shall I propose on my part, O men of Athens? Clearly that which is my due. And what is that which I ought to pay or to receive? What shall be done to the man who has never had the wit to be idle during his whole life; but has been careless of what the many care about — wealth, and family interests, and military offices, and speaking in the assembly, and magistracies, and plots, and parties? Reflecting that I was really too honest a man to follow in this way and live, I did not go where I could do no good to you or to myself; but where I could do the greatest good privately to every one of you, thither I went, and sought to persuade every man among you that he must look to himself, and seek virtue and wisdom before he looks to his private interests, and look to the state before he looks to the interests of the state; and that this should be the order which he observes in all his actions. What shall be done to such an one? Doubtless some good thing, O men of Athens, if he has his reward; and the good should be of a kind suitable to him. What would be a reward suitable to a poor man who is your benefactor, who desires leisure that he may instruct you? There can be no more fitting reward than maintenance in the Prytaneum, O men of Athens, a reward which he deserves far more than the citizen who has won the prize at Olympia in the horse or chariot race, whether the chariots were drawn by two horses or by many. For I am in want, and he has enough; and he only gives you the appearance of happiness, and I give you the reality. And if I am to estimate the penalty fairly, I should say that maintenance in the Prytaneum is the just return.

Perhaps you think that I am braving you in what I am saying now, as in what I said before about the tears and prayers. But this is not the case. I speak rather because I am convinced that I never intentionally wronged any one, although I cannot convince you of that — for we have had a short conversation only; but if there were a law in Athens, such as there is in other cities, that a capital cause should not be decided in one day, then I believe that I should have convinced you; but now the time is too short. I cannot in a moment refute great slanders; and as I am convinced that I never wronged another, I will assuredly not wrong myself. I will not say of myself that I deserve any evil, or propose any penalty. Why should I? Because I am afraid of the penalty of death, which Meletus proposes? When I do not know whether death is a good or an evil, why should I propose a penalty which would certainly be an evil? Shall I say imprisonment? And why should I live in prison, and be the slave of the magistrates of the year — of the Eleven? Or shall the penalty be a fine, and imprisonment until the fine is paid? There is the same objection. I should have to lie in prison, for money I have none, and cannot pay. And if I say exile (and this may possibly be the penalty which you will affix), I must indeed be blinded by the love of life if I am so irrational as to expect that when you, who are my own citizens, cannot endure my discourses and words, and have found them so grievous and odious that you would fain have done with them, others are likely to endure me. No, indeed, men of Athens, that is not very likely. And what a life should I lead, at my age, wandering from city to city, living in ever-changing exile, and always being driven out! For I am quite sure that into whatever place I go, as here so also there, the young men will come and listen to me; and if I drive them away, their elders will drive me out at their desire; and if I let them come, their fathers and friends will drive me out for their sakes.

Some one will say: Yes, Socrates, but cannot you hold your tongue, and then you may go into a foreign city, and no one will interfere with you? Now I have great difficulty in making you understand my answer to this. For if I tell you that to do as you say would be a disobedience to the God, and therefore that I cannot hold my tongue, you will not believe that I am serious; and if I say again that the greatest good of man is daily to converse about virtue and all that concerning which you hear me examining myself and others, and that the life which is unexamined is not worth living, you are still less likely to believe me. And yet what I say is indeed true, although a thing of which it is hard for me to persuade you. Moreover I have not been accustomed to think that I deserve any punishment. Had I money I might have estimated the offence at what I was able to pay, and have been none the worse.

But you see that I have none, and I can only ask you to proportion the fine to my means. However, I think that I could afford a mina, and therefore I propose that penalty. Plato, Crito, Critobulus, and Apollodorus, my friends here, bid me say thirty minæ, and they will be the sureties. Well, then, say thirty minæ, and let that be the penalty; and for that sum they will be ample security to you.

[The judges now proceeded to pass the sentence, and condemned Socrates to death; whereupon he continued : —]

Not much time will be gained, O Athenians, in return for the evil name which you will get from the detractors of the city, who will say that you killed Socrates, a wise man ; for they will call me wise, even although I am not wise, when they want to reproach you. If you had waited a little, while, your desire would have been fulfilled in the course of nature. For I am far advanced in years, as you may perceive, and not far from death. I am speaking now only to those of you who have condemned me to death. And I have another thing to say to them : You think that I was convicted because I had no words of the sort that would have procured my acquittal — I mean, if I had thought fit to leave nothing undone or unsaid. Not so; the deficiency which led to my conviction was not of words, — certainly not. But I had not the boldness or impudence or inclination to address you as you would have liked me to address you, weeping and wailing and lamenting, and saying and doing many things which you have been accustomed to hear from others, and which, as I maintain, are unworthy of me. I thought at the time that I ought not to do anything common or mean when in danger; nor do I now repent of the manner of my defence, and I would rather die having spoken after my manner, than speak in your manner and live. For neither in war nor yet at law ought I or any man to use every way of escaping death. Often in battle there can be no doubt that if a man will throw away his arms, and fall on his knees before his pursuers, he may escape death; and in other dangers there are other ways of escaping death, if a man is willing to say and do anything. The difficulty, my friends, is not in avoiding death, but in avoiding unrighteousness; for that runs faster than death. I am old, and move slowly, and the slower runner has overtaken me, and my accusers are keen and quick, and the faster runner, who is unrighteousness, has overtaken them. And now I depart hence condemned by you to suffer the penalty of death; and they too go their ways condemned by the truth to suffer the penalty of villany and wrong; and I must abide by my award — let them abide by theirs. I suppose that these things may be regarded as fated, — and I think that they are well.

And now, O men who have condemned me, I would fain prophesy to you; for I am about to die, and that is the hour in which men are gifted with prophetic power. And I prophesy to you who are my murderers, that immediately after my death punishment far heavier than you have inflicted on me will surely await you. Me you have killed because you wanted to escape the accuser, and not to give an account of your lives. But that will not be as you suppose; far otherwise. For I say that there will be more accusers of you than there are now; accusers whom hitherto I have restrained: and as they are younger they will be more inconsiderate with you, and you will be more offended at them. If you think that by killing men you can prevent some one from censuring your evil lives, you are mistaken: that is not a way of escape which is either possible or honorable; the easiest and the noblest way is not to be disabling others, but to be improving yourselves. This is the prophecy which I utter before my departure to the judges who have condemned me.

Friends, who would have acquitted me, I would like also to talk with you about this thing which has happened, while the magistrates are busy, and before I go to the place at which I must die. Stay then awhile, for we may as well talk with one another while there is time. You are my friends, and I should like to show you the meaning of this event which has happened to me. O my judges — for you I may truly call judges — I should like to tell you of a wonderful circumstance. Hitherto the familiar oracle within me has constantly been in the habit of opposing me even about trifles, if I was going to make a slip or error in any matter: and now, as you see, there has come upon me that which may be thought, and is generally believed to be, the last and worst evil. But the oracle made no sign of opposition, either as I was leaving my house and going out in the morning, or when I was going up into this court, or while I was speaking, at anything which I was going to say; and yet I have often been stopped in the middle of a speech. But now in nothing I either said or did touching this matter has the oracle opposed me. What do I take to be the explanation of this? I will tell you. I regard this as a great proof that what has happened to me is a good, and that those of us who think that death is an evil are in error. For the customary sign would surely have opposed me had I been going to evil, and not to good.

Let us reflect in another way, and we shall see that there is great reason to hope that death is a good; for one of two things — either death is a state of nothingness and utter unconsciousness, or, as men say, there is a change and migration of the soul from this world to another. Now if you suppose that there is no consciousness, but a sleep like the sleep of him who is undisturbed even by the sight of dreams, death will be an unspeakable gain. For if a person were to select the night in which his sleep was undisturbed even by dreams, and were to compare with this the other days and nights of his life, and then were to tell us how many days and nights he had passed in the course of his life better and more pleasantly than this one, I think that any man, I will not say a private man, but even the great king will not find many such days or nights, when compared with the others. Now if death is like this, I say that to die is gain; for eternity is then only a single night. But if death is the journey to another place, and there, as men say, all the dead are, what good, O my friends and judges, can be greater than this? If indeed when the pilgrim arrives in the world below, he is delivered from the professors of justice in this world, and finds the true judges who are said to give judgment there, Minos and Rhadamanthus and Æacus and Triptolemus, and other sons of God who were righteous in their own life, that pilgrimage will be worth making. What would not a man give if he might converse with Orpheus and Musæus and Hesiod and Homer? Nay, if this be true, let me die again and again. I myself, too, shall have a wonderful interest in there meeting and conversing with Palamedes, and Ajax the son of Telamon, and other heroes of old, who have suffered death through an unjust judgment; and there will be no small pleasure, as I think,

Apology.   71

in comparing my own sufferings with theirs. Above all, I shall then be able to continue my search into true and false knowledge; as in this world, so also in that; and I shall find out who is wise, and who pretends to be wise, and is not. What would not a man give, O judges, to be able to examine the leader of the great Trojan expedition; or Odysseus or Sisyphus, or numberless others, men and women too! What infinite delight would there be in conversing with them and asking them questions! In another world they do not put a man to death for asking questions; assuredly not. For besides being happier in that world than in this, they will be immortal, if what is said is true.

Wherefore, O judges, be of good cheer about death, and know of a certainty, that no evil can happen to a good man, either in life or after death. He and his are not neglected by the gods: nor has my own approaching end happened by mere chance. But I see clearly that to die and be released was better for me; and therefore the oracle gave no sign. For which reason, also, I am not angry with my condemners, or with my accusers; they have done me no harm, although they did not mean to do me any good; and for this I may gently blame them.

Still I have a favor to ask of them. When my sons are grown up, I would ask you, O my friends, to punish them; and I would have you trouble them, as I have troubled you, if they seem to care about riches, or anything, more than about virtue; or if they pretend to be something when they are really nothing, — then reprove them, as I have reproved you, for not caring about that for which they ought to care, and thinking that they are something when they are really nothing. And if you do this, I and my sons will have received justice at your hands.

The hour of departure has arrived, and we go our ways — I to die, and you to live. Which is better God only knows.

Crito.

PERSONS OF THE DIALOGUE.

SOCRATES.   CRITO.

SCENE:— *The Prison of Socrates.*

SOCRATES. Why have you come at this hour, Crito? It must be quite early?

CRITO. Yes, certainly.

Soc. What is the exact time?

CR. The dawn is breaking.

Soc. I wonder that the keeper of the prison would let you in.

CR. He knows me, because I often come, Socrates; moreover, I have done him a kindness.

Soc. And are you only just arrived?

CR. No, I came some time ago.

Soc. Then why did you sit and say nothing, instead of at once awakening me?

CR. By the gods, Socrates, I would rather

not myself have all this sleeplessness and sorrow. And I have been wondering at your peaceful slumbers, which was the reason why I did not awaken you, because I wanted you to be out of pain. I have always thought you of a happy disposition; but never did I see anything like the easy, tranquil manner in which you bear this calamity.

Soc. Why, Crito, when a man has reached my age he ought not to be repining at the prospect of death.

Cr. And yet other old men find themselves in similar misfortunes, and age does not prevent them from repining.

Soc. That may be. But you have not told me why you come at this early hour.

Cr. I come to bring you a message which is sad and painful; not, as I believe, to yourself, but to all of us who are your friends, and saddest of all to me.

Soc. What? Has the ship come from Delos, on the arrival of which I am to die?

Cr. No, the ship has not actually arrived, but she will probably be here to-day, as persons who have come from Sunium tell me that they left her there; and therefore to-morrow, Socrates, will be the last day of your life.

Soc. Very well, Crito; if such is the will of God, I am willing; but my belief is that there will be a delay of a day.

Cr. Why do you think so?

Soc. I will tell you. I am to die on the day after the arrival of the ship?

Cr. Yes; that is what the authorities say.

Soc. But I do not think that the ship will be here until to-morrow; this I infer from a vision which I had last night, or rather only just now, when you fortunately allowed me to sleep.

Cr. And what was the nature of the vision?

Soc. There came to me the likeness of a woman, fair and comely, clothed in white raiment, who called to me and said: "O Socrates,

"'The third day hence to Phthia shalt thou go.'"[1]

Cr. What a singular dream, Socrates!

Soc. There can be no doubt about the meaning, Crito, I think.

Cr. Yes; the meaning is only too clear. But oh! my beloved Socrates, let me entreat you once more to take my advice and escape. For if you die I shall not only lose a friend

[1] Homer, Il. ix. 363.

who can never be replaced, but there is another evil: people who do not know you and me will believe that I might have saved you if I had been willing to give money, but that I did not care. Now, can there be a worse disgrace than this — that I should be thought to value money more than the life of a friend? For the many will not be persuaded that I wanted you to escape and that you refused.

Soc. But why, my dear Crito, should we care about the opinion of the many? Good men, and they are the only persons who are worth considering, will think of these things truly as they occurred.

Cr. But you see, Socrates, that the opinion of the many must be regarded, for what is now happening shows that they can do the greatest evil to any one who has lost their good opinion.

Soc. I only wish, Crito, that they could; for then they could also do the greatest good, and that would be well. But in reality they can do neither; for they cannot either make a man wise or make him foolish; and whatever they do is the result of chance.

Cr. Well, I will not dispute with you; but please to tell me, Socrates, whether you are not acting out of regard to me and your other friends: are you not afraid that if you escape from prison we may get into trouble with the informers for having stolen you away, and lose either the whole or a great part of our property; or that even a worse evil may happen to us? Now, if this is your fear, be at ease; for in order to save you, we ought surely to run this, or even a greater risk; be persuaded, then, and do as I say.

Soc. Yes, Crito, that is one fear which you mention, but by no means the only one.

Cr. Fear not. There are persons who at no great cost are willing to save you and bring you out of prison; and as for the informers, they are far from being exorbitant in their demands; you may observe that a little money will satisfy them. My means, which are certainly ample, are at your service, and if you have a scruple about spending all mine, here are strangers who will give you the use of theirs; and one of them, Simmias the Theban, has brought a sum of money for this very purpose; and Cebes and many others are willing to spend their money too. I say, therefore, do not on that account hesitate about making your escape, and do not say, as you did in the court, that you will have a difficulty in knowing what to do with yourself if you escape. For men will love you in other places to which you may go, and not in Athens only; there are friends of mine in Thessaly, if you like to go to them, who will value and protect you, and no Thessalian will give you any trouble. Nor can I think that you are justified, Socrates, in betraying your own life when you might be saved: this is playing into the hands of your enemies and destroyers; and further, I should say that you were deserting your own children; for you might bring them up and educate them, instead of which you go away and leave them; and they will have to take their chance; and if they do not meet with the usual fate of orphans, there will be small thanks to you. No man should bring children into the world who is unwilling to persevere to the end in their nurture and education. But you appear to be choosing the easier part, not the better and manlier, which would rather have become one who professes to care for virtue in all his actions, like yourself. And indeed, I am ashamed not only of you, but of us who are your friends, when I reflect that this affair of yours will be attributed entirely to our want of courage. The trial need never have come on, or might have been managed differently; and this last act, or crowning folly, will seem to have occurred through our neglect and cowardice, who might have saved you, if we had been good for anything, as you might have saved yourself, for there was no difficulty at all. See now, Socrates, how sad and dishonorable are the consequences, both to us and you. Make up your mind then, or rather have your mind already made up, for the time of deliberation is over, and there is only one thing to be done, which must be done this very night, and if we delay at all will be no longer practicable or possible; I beseech you therefore, Socrates, be persuaded by me, and do as I say.

Soc. Dear Crito, your zeal is invaluable, if a right one; but if wrong, the greater the zeal the greater the danger; and therefore we ought to consider whether I shall or shall not do as you say. For I am and always have been one of those natures who must be guided by reason, whatever the reason may be which upon reflection appears to me to be the best; and now that this fortune has come upon me,

I cannot put away the conclusion at which I had arrived: the principles which I have hitherto honored and revered I still honor, and unless we can at once find other and better principles, I am certain not to agree with you; no, not even if the power of the multitude could inflict many more imprisonments, confiscations, deaths, frightening us like children with hobgoblin terrors. But what will be the fairest way of considering the question? Shall I return to your old argument about the opinions of men? some of which are to be regarded, and others, as we were saying, are not to be regarded. Now were we right in maintaining this before I was condemned? And has the argument which was once good now proved to be talk for the sake of talking;—in fact an amusement only, and altogether vanity? That is what I want to consider with your help, Crito;—whether, under my present circumstances, the argument appears to be in any way different or not; and is to be allowed by me or disallowed. That argument, which, as I believe, is maintained by many who assume to be authorities, was to the effect, as I was saying, that the opinions of some men are to be regarded, and of other men not to be regarded. Now you, Crito, are a disinterested person who are not going to die to-morrow — at least, there is no human probability of this, and you are therefore not liable to be deceived by the circumstances in which you are placed. Tell me then, whether I am right in saying that some opinions, and the opinions of some men only, are to be valued, and that other opinions, and the opinions of other men, are not to be valued. I ask you whether I was right in maintaining this?

Cr. Certainly.

Soc. The good are to be regarded, and not the bad?

Cr. Yes.

Soc. And the opinions of the wise are good, and the opinions of the unwise are evil?

Cr. Certainly.

Soc. And what was said about another matter? Was the disciple in gymnastics supposed to attend to the praise and blame and opinion of every man, or of one man only, — his physician or trainer, whoever that was?

Cr. Of one man only.

Soc. And he ought to fear the censure and welcome the praise of that one only, and not of the many?

Cr. That is clear.

Soc. And he ought to act and train, and eat and drink in the way which seems good to his single master who has understanding, rather than according to the opinions of all other men put together?

Cr. True.

Soc. And if he disobeys and disregards the opinion and approval of the one, and regards the opinion of the many who have no understanding, will he not suffer evil?

Cr. Certainly he will.

Soc. And what will the evil be, whither tending and what affecting, in the disobedient person?

Cr. Clearly affecting the body: that is what is destroyed by the evil.

Soc. Very good; and is not this true, Crito, of other things which we need not separately enumerate? In questions of just and unjust, fair and foul, good and evil, which are the subjects of our present consultation, ought we to follow the opinion of the many and to fear them; or the opinion of the one man who has understanding? Ought we not to fear and reverence him more than all the rest of the world: and if we desert him shall we not destroy and injure that principle in us which may be assumed to be improved by justice and deteriorated by injustice; there is such a principle?

CR. Certainly there is, Socrates.

Soc. Take a parallel instance: — if, acting under the advice of men who have no understanding, we destroy that which is improved by health and is deteriorated by disease, would life be worth having? And that which has been destroyed is — the body?

CR. Yes.

Soc. Could we live, having an evil and corrupted body?

CR. Certainly not.

Soc. And will life be worth having, if that higher part of man be destroyed, which is improved by justice and deteriorated by injustice? Do we suppose that principle, whatever it may be in man, which has to do with justice and injustice, to be inferior to the body?

CR. Certainly not.

Soc. More honored, then?

CR. Far more honored.

Soc. Then, my friend, we must not regard what the many say of us: but what he, the one man who has understanding of just and unjust, will say, and what the truth will say. And therefore you begin in error when you advise that we should regard the opinion of the many about just and unjust, good and evil, honorable and dishonorable. — " Well," some one will say, " but the many can kill us."

Cr. Yes, Socrates, that will clearly be the answer.

Soc. That is true; but still I find with surprise that the old argument is, as I conceive, unshaken as ever. And I should like to know whether I may say the same of another proposition — that not life, but a good life, is to be chiefly valued?

Cr. Yes, that also remains.

Soc. And a good life is equivalent to a just and honorable one — that holds also?

Cr. Yes, that holds.

Soc. From these premisses I proceed to argue the question whether I ought or ought not to try and escape without the consent of the Athenians: and if I am clearly right in escaping, then I will make the attempt; but if not, I will abstain. The other considerations which you mention, of money and the loss of character and the duty of educating one's children are, I fear, only the doctrines of the multitude, who would be as ready to call people to life, if they were able, as they are to put them to death — and with as little reason. But now, since the argument has thus far prevailed, the only question which remains to be considered is, whether we shall do rightly either in escaping or in suffering others to aid in our escape and paying them in money and thanks, or whether we shall not do rightly; and if the latter, then death or any other calamity which may ensue on my remaining here must not be allowed to enter into the calculation.

CR. I think that you are right, Socrates; how then shall we proceed?

Soc. Let us consider the matter together, and do you either refute me if you can, and I will be convinced; or else cease, my dear friend, from repeating to me that I ought to escape against the wishes of the Athenians: for I am extremely desirous to be persuaded by you, but not against my own better judgment. And now please to consider my first position, and try how you can best answer me.

CR. I will.

Soc. Are we to say that we are never intentionally to do wrong, or that in one way we ought and in another way we ought not to do wrong, or is doing wrong always evil and dishonorable, as I was just now saying, and as has been already acknowledged by us? Are all our former admissions which were made within a few days to be thrown away? And have we, at our age, been earnestly discoursing with one another all our life long only to discover that we are no better than children? Or, in spite of the opinion of the many, and in spite of consequences whether better or worse, shall we insist on the truth of what was then said, that injustice is always an evil and dishonor to him who acts unjustly? Shall we say so or not?

Cr. Yes.

Soc. Then we must do no wrong?

Cr. Certainly not.

Soc. Nor when injured injure in return, as the many imagine; for we must injure no one at all?

Cr. Clearly not.

Soc. Again, Crito, may we do evil?

Cr. Surely not, Socrates.

Soc. And what of doing evil in return for

evil, which is the morality of the many — is that just or not?

CR. Not just.

Soc. For doing evil to another is the same as injuring him?

CR. Very true.

Soc. Then we ought not to retaliate or render evil for evil to any one, whatever evil we may have suffered from him. But I would have you consider, Crito, whether you really mean what you are saying. For this opinion has never been held, and never will be held by any considerable number of persons; and those who are agreed and those who are not agreed upon this point have no common ground, and can only despise one another when they see how widely they differ. Tell me, then, whether you agree with and assent to my first principle, that neither injury nor retaliation nor warding off evil by evil is ever right. And shall that be the premiss of our argument? Or do you decline and dissent from this? For thus I have ever thought, and still think; but, if you are of another opinion, let me hear what you have to say. If, however, you remain of the same mind as formerly, I will proceed to the next step.

CR. You may proceed, for I have not changed my mind.

Soc. Then I will proceed to the next step, which may be put in the form of a question: — Ought a man to do what he admits to be right, or ought he to betray the right?

CR. He ought to do what he thinks right.

Soc. But if this is true, what is the application? In leaving the prison against the will of the Athenians, do I wrong any? or rather do I not wrong those whom I ought least to wrong? Do I not desert the principles which were acknowledged by us to be just — what do you say?

CR. I cannot tell, Socrates; for I do not know.

Soc. Then consider the matter in this way: — Imagine that I am about to play truant (you may call the proceeding by any name which you like), and the laws and the government come and interrogate me: "Tell us, Socrates," they say; "what are you about? are you going by an act of yours to overturn us — the laws, and the whole state, as far as in you lies? Do you imagine that a state can subsist and not be overthrown, in which the decisions of law have no power, but are set aside and overthrown by individuals?" What will be our answer, Crito, to these and the like words? Any one, and especially a rhetorician, will have a good deal to say on behalf of the law which requires a sentence to be carried out; —he will argue that this law should not be set aside; and we might reply, "Yes; but the state has injured us and given an unjust sentence." Suppose I say that?

CR. Very good, Socrates.

Soc. "And was that our agreement with you?" the law would reply; "or were you to abide by the sentence of the state?" And if I were to express my astonishment at their words, the law would probably add: "Answer, Socrates, instead of opening your eyes: you are in the habit of asking and answering questions. Tell us what complaint you have to make against us which justifies you in attempting to destroy us and the state? In the first place did we not bring you into existence? Your father married your mother by our aid and begat you. Say whether you have any objection to urge against those of us who regulate marriage?" None, I should reply. "Or against those of us who after birth regulate the nurture and education of children, in which you also were trained? Were not the laws, which have the charge of education, right in commanding your father to train you in music and gymnastic?" Right, I should reply. "Well then, since you were brought into the world and nurtured and educated by us, can you deny in the first place that you are our child and slave, as your fathers were before you? And if this is true you are not on equal terms with us; nor can you think that you have a right to do to us what we are doing to you. Would you have any right to strike or revile or do any other evil to your father or your master, if you had one, because you have been struck or reviled by him, or received some other evil at his hands? — you would not say this? And because we think right to destroy you, do you think that you have any right to destroy us in return, and your country as far as in you lies? Will you, O professor of true virtue, pretend that you are justified in this? Has a philosopher like you failed to discover that our country is more to be valued and higher and holier far than mother or father or any ancestor, and more to be regarded in the eyes of the gods and of men of understanding?

also to be soothed, and gently and reverently entreated when angry, even more than a father, and if not persuaded, obeyed? And when we are punished by her, whether with imprisonment or stripes, the punishment is to be endured in silence; and if she leads us to wounds or death in battle, thither we follow as is right: neither may any one yield or retreat or leave his rank, but whether in battle or in a court of law, or in any other place, he must do what his city or his country order him; or he must change their view of what is just: and if he may do no violence to his father or mother, much less may he do violence to his country." What answer shall we make to this, Crito? Do the laws speak truly, or do they not?

CR. I think that they do.

SOC. Then the laws will say: "Consider, Socrates, if we are speaking truly that in your present attempt you are going to do us an injury. For, after having brought you into the world, and nurtured and educated you, and given you and every other citizen a share in every good which we had to give, we further proclaim to every Athenian, that if he does not like us when he has come of age and has seen the ways of the city, and made our acquaintance, he may go where he pleases and take his goods with him; and none of us laws will forbid him or interfere with him. Any of you who does not like us and the city, and who wants to emigrate to a colony or to any other city, may go where he likes, and take his goods with him. But he who has experience of the manner in which we order justice and administer the state, and still remains, has entered into an implied contract that he will do as we command him. And he who disobeys us, is, as we maintain, thrice wrong; first, because in disobeying us, he is disobeying his parents; secondly, because we are the authors of his education; thirdly, because he has made an agreement with us that he will duly obey our commands; and he neither obeys them nor convinces us that our commands are unjust; and we do not rudely impose them, but give him the alternative of obeying or convincing us;—that is what we offer, and he does neither. These are the sort of accusations to which, as we were saying, you, Socrates, will be exposed if you accomplish your intentions; you, above all other Athenians." Suppose I ask, why is this? they will justly retort upon me that I above all other men have acknowledged the agreement. "There is clear proof," they will say, "Socrates, that we and the city were not displeasing to you. Of all Athenians you have been the most constant resident in the city, which, as you never leave, you may be supposed to love. For you never went out of the city either to see the games, except once when you went to the Isthmus, or to any other place unless when you were on military service; nor did you travel as other men do. Nor had you any curiosity to know other states or their laws: your affections did not go beyond us and our state; we were your special favorites, and you acquiesced in our government of you; and here in this city you begat your children, which is a proof of your satisfaction. Moreover you might, if you had liked, have fixed the penalty at banishment in the course of the trial — the state which refuses to let you go now would have let you go then. But you pretended that you preferred death to exile, and that you were not grieved at death. And now you have forgotten these fine sentiments, and pay no respect to us the laws, of whom you are the destroyer; and are doing what only a miserable slave would do, running away and turning your back upon the compacts and agreements which you made as a citizen. And first of all answer this very question: Are we right in saying that you agreed to be governed according to us in deed and not in word only? Is that true, or not?" How shall we answer, Crito? Must we not assent?

CR. There is no help, Socrates.

SOC. Then will they not say: "You, Socrates, are breaking the covenants and agreements which you made with us at your leisure, not in any haste or under any compulsion or deception, but having had seventy years to think of them, during which time you were at liberty to leave the city, if we were not to your mind, or if our covenants appeared to you to be unfair. You had your choice, and might have gone either to Lacedæmon or Crete, which you often praise for their good government, or to some other Hellenic or foreign state. Whereas you, above all other Athenians, seemed to be so fond of the state, or, in other words, of us her laws (for who would like a state that has no laws?), that you never stirred out of her; the halt, the blind, the maimed, were not more stationary in her than you were. And now you run away and for-

Crito.

sake your agreements. Not so, Socrates, if you will take our advice; do not make yourself ridiculous by escaping out of the city.

"For just consider, if you transgress and err in this sort of way, what good will you do either to yourself or to your friends? That your friends will be driven into exile and deprived of citizenship, or will lose their property, is tolerably certain; and you yourself, if you fly to one of the neighboring cities, as, for example, Thebes or Megara, both of which are well-governed cities, will come to them as an enemy, Socrates, and their government will be against you, and all patriotic citizens will cast an evil eye upon you as a subverter of the laws, and you will confirm in the minds of the judges the justice of their own condemnation of you. For he who is a corrupter of the laws is more than likely to be a corrupter of the young and foolish portion of mankind. Will you then flee from well-ordered cities and virtuous men? And is existence worth having on these terms? Or will you go to them without shame and talk to them, Socrates? And what will you say to them? What you say here about virtue and justice and institutions and laws being the best things among men? Would that be decent of you? Surely not. But if you go away from well-governed states to Crito's friends in Thessaly, where there is great disorder and license, they will be charmed to have the tale of your escape from prison, set off with ludicrous particulars of the manner in which you were wrapped in a goatskin or some other disguise, and metamorphosed as the manner of runaways is — that is very likely; but will there be no one to remind you that in your old age you were not ashamed to violate the most sacred laws from a miserable desire of a little more life? Perhaps not, if you keep them in a good temper; but if they are out of temper you will hear many degrading things: you will live, but how? — as the flatterer of all men, and the servant of all men; and doing what? — eating and drinking in Thessaly, having gone abroad in order that you may get a dinner. And where will be your fine sentiments about justice and virtue then? Say that you wish to live for the sake of your children, that you may bring them up and educate them — will you take them into Thessaly and deprive them of Athenian citizenship? Is that the benefit which you would confer upon them? Or are you under the impression that they will be better cared for and educated here if you are still alive, although absent from them; for that your friends will take care of them? Do you fancy that if you are an inhabitant of Thessaly they will take care of them, and if you are an inhabitant of the other world that they will not take care of them? Nay; but if they who call themselves friends are good for anything, they surely will.

"Listen then, Socrates, to us who have brought you up. Think not of life and children first, and of justice afterwards, but of justice first, that you may be justified before the princes of the world below. For neither will you nor any that belong to you be happier or holier or juster in this life, or happier in another, if you do as Crito bids. Now you depart in innocence, a sufferer and not a doer of evil; a victim not of the laws but of men. But if you go forth, returning evil for evil, and injury for injury, breaking the covenants and agreements which you have made with us, and wronging those whom you ought least to wrong, that is to say, yourself, your friends, your country, and us, we shall be angry with you while you live, and our brethren, the laws in the world below, will receive you as an enemy; for they will know that you have done your best to destroy us. Listen, then, to us, and not to Crito."

This is the voice which I seem to hear murmuring in my ears, like the sound of the flute in the ears of the mystic; that voice, I say, is humming in my ears, and prevents me from hearing any other. And I know that anything more which you may say will be vain. Yet speak, if you have anything to say.

CR. I have nothing to say, Socrates.

SOC. Leave me then to follow whithersoever God leads.

www.ingramcontent.com/pod-product-compliance
Lightning Source LLC
Chambersburg PA
CBHW030411170426
43202CB00010B/1565